# THE GREAT BOOK OF ANIMAL KNOWLEDGE

# MOOSE

## Largest Deer in the World

All Rights Reserved. All written content in this book may NOT be reproduced in any form or by any means, including scanning, photocopying, or otherwise without prior written permission of the copyright holder. Copyright © 2014

Some Rights Reserved. All photographs contained in this book are under the Creative Commons license and can be copied and redistributed in any medium or format for any purpose, even commercially. However, you must give appropriate credit, provide a link to the license, and indicate if changes were made.

# Introduction

Photo by Denali National Park and Preserve (flickr.com/denalinps), as licensed under CC BY 2.0 Generic

The moose is the largest member of the deer family. They are big, strong and have large antlers. There are a lot of moose scattered all around the colder parts of the northern hemisphere. Let's learn more about the largest deer in the world!

# What Moose Look Like

Moose have big bodies and long, skinny legs. They have a hump in their back and a flap of skin hanging from their throat called a bell. Male moose have large, wide, and flat antlers. Normally females don't grow antlers. It is very rare for a female to have antlers. Moose also have a very short tail.

# Size and Weight

Photo by Fisherga (flickr.com/gailfisher), as licensed under CC BY 2.0 Generic

Moose are very big animals. They are the largest members of the deer family! They are also the tallest mammals in North America. Their height, from hoof to shoulders, can grow up to 6.5 feet tall! Moose are also very heavy. They weigh around 1,800 pounds! Male moose are heavier than females.

# Antlers

Male moose have very large, broad antlers that can grow up to 6 ft wide! Antlers look like a palm of a hand with outstretched fingers. Moose use antlers to attract mates, scare off other males, or even to fight with each other! Every year, male moose go through an antler cycle. Moose start growing antlers when they reach one year old. Antlers grow covered in a furry tissue called velvet during the spring. The velvet falls off once the antler is fully grown and before the mating season. Moose usually shed their horns before winter to save energy. Then when spring arrives the cycle is repeated.

# Velvet

Unlike horns, the antlers of moose needs blood and nutrients to grow. Antlers grow covered in a tissue called velvet. The furry velvet supplies the antler with the blood and the nutrients it needs. When the antler has fully grown the velvet will dry and start to fall off. Moose will often rub their antlers on trees to help remove the velvet.

# Legs and Hooves

Photo by Andrew E. Russell (flickr.com/25949441@N02), as licensed under CC BY 2.0 Generic

The front legs of a moose are longer than their hind legs. This helps them jump over things lying in their path. Moose can kick very hard with their legs. They try to fight off predators by kicking them with their sharp hooves. Moose kick with their front and hind legs in any direction! So there is no safe side to approach a moose. The hooves of a moose also act like snowshoes; they help the moose walk easily even in thick snow!

# Bell

The beard-like structure on the throat of a moose is called a bell. The bell grows larger as the moose gets older. The actual use of the bell is still unknown. Some scientists think it's for attracting mates. While others think it's for keeping a regular temperature during summer or keeping the throat warm during winter. It might also be used for communicating to other moose.

# Senses

Moose have pretty poor eyesight. The eyes of a moose are located more on the sides of their head so they have a big blind spot in front of them. Moose have a very good sense of smell. Their sense of smell is much better than a human's sense of smell. They also have a good sense of hearing.

# What Moose Eat

Moose are herbivores, which means that they only eat plants and plant material. Moose need to eat a lot due to their large size. They like eating leaves, buds, shrubs, and low lying plants. During summer, moose like to swim in lakes and eat the floating pond lilies. Moose also eat twigs, in fact, the word moose means "twig eater." They also like to strip off bark from trees and eat the bark!

# Swimming

Moose are excellent swimmers. During summer, moose often swim in lakes to eat water plants, escape flies or a pack of wolves, or simply to relax in the water. Moose can swim 6 miles per hour for a long period of time. Baby moose can also swim because moose are born with the ability to swim.

# What Moose Do

Moose are solitary animals, each moose lives on their own. The only time moose stay together is during mating season or a mother raising her young. Moose are most active during sunrise and sunset. They spend most of their time eating, looking for new grazing spots, or just resting.

# Where Moose Live

Photo by Martin Cathrae (flickr.com/suckamc), as licensed under CC BY-SA 2.0 Generic

Moose can be found almost anywhere in the northern parts of the world; North America, Russia, northern Europe, and there are a few moose in Mongolia and China. Moose live in places with seasonal snow cover. They can't survive hot climates because they can't sweat.

# Sounds

During the mating season, moose will call out to each other. Male moose produce heavy grunting sounds that can be heard more than 500 yards away. Female moose produce a wail-like sound.

# Fighting Each Other

Moose usually fight each other during the mating season. The mating season occurs on September and October. Some male moose will gather a herd of females to mate with. Other males will fight the leader of the herd for the right to mate. Moose fight each other by going head to head with their antlers. Most of the time these fights end quickly with no one getting injured, but sometimes the antlers of the two moose get so entangled that they both die! Moose don't just use their antlers for fighting other males. Sometimes they use it to scare off younger males with smaller antlers.

# Baby Moose

Photo by Shanna Waller (flickr.com/shannamae), as licensed under CC BY-SA 2.0 Generic

Female moose will usually give birth to only one calf, although sometimes, if the food is plenty, they give birth to two calves. The fur of a baby moose is a little redder than the brown fur of an adult moose. Sadly, most moose die when they are not yet fully grown. Predators like to hunt young and defenseless baby moose.

# Life of a Moose

Baby moose learn to walk in less than a day but their mother will have to protect them from predators. A baby moose will stay with its mother until it reaches one year old. After a year, the mother will chase away her young one before giving birth again so she can focus on her new calf. The year old moose will then go away and live on its own. If moose survive up to maturity they will usually live up to 15-25 years.

# Predators

Photo by Dana Moos (flickr.com/dana_moos), as licensed under CC BY 2.0 Generic

A fully grown moose doesn't have many predators. Their only real threats are Siberian tigers and a pack of wolves. Young moose, however, are preyed by many different predators including bears and cougars. Sometimes, when moose are swimming between islands, killer whales kill and eat them! Moose try to avoid predators by using their strong sense of smell and hearing. If a predator finds them, they will sometimes stand ground and try to kick their predator as hard as they can. Moose can fight off bears by kicking and although a moose can't really fight a pack of wolves, kicking makes them a less preferred prey.

# Speed

Moose don't always stand ground and fight against wolves. Many times, when they sense a pack of wolves, they will try to run away. Moose are fast runners; they can run up to 35 miles per hour!

# Aggression

Photo by Dave Bezaire & Susi Havens-Bezaire (flickr.com/ dlbezaire), as licensed under CC BY-SA 2.0 Generic

Moose don't normally attack humans. But if a human startles or frightens them they will charge at the human! Moose display their aggression by maintaining eye contact, lowering their head, and the raising the hair on the back of their neck. A surprising fact about moose is that they actually attack more humans than wolves and bears combined! But the attacks of a moose usually have only small consequences.

# Humans and Moose

Humans have hunted moose for a very, very long time already. Carvings of people hunting moose were found in ancient caves. Today people still hunt, and eat moose. Hunters often cut off the head of a moose and keep it as a trophy. Sometimes, moose and vehicles collide. When the car hits the moose the moose will crash on the windshield of the car and into the front seats. Moose and vehicle collisions are deadly for both the moose and the driver of the car.

# Subspecies

There are several subspecies of moose. There are only very small differences between subspecies. The biggest difference is where they are found. The subspecies of moose are Eurasian elk, Yakutia moose, Amur moose, Chukotka moose, Eastern moose, Western moose, Alaska moose, Shiras moose, and the now extinct Caucasian moose.

# Get the next book in this series!

## MEERKATS: Standing Sentires of the Mongoose Family

Log on to Facebook.com/GazelleCB for more info

Tip: Use the key-phrase "The Great Book of Animal Knowledge" when searching for books in this series.

For more information about our books, discounts and updates, please Like us on Facebook!

Facebook.com/GazelleCB

Made in the USA
Middletown, DE
12 February 2020